To our Sourdough friends at Barrow with lots of good wishes Mel & Olivia _____

MY SOURDOUGH DAD

The term "Sourdough" is given to one who spends one or more winters in Alaska. Such a person is given much more respect by the Eskimo than one whom they call "Cheechako". A Cheechako is a person who has never wintered in Alaska.

MY

SOURDOUGH

DAD

Olivia Casberg

THE OLIVE PRESS PUBLICATIONS

Library of Congress Cataloging-in-Publication Data

Casberg, Olivia, 1910-
    My sourdough dad, 1877-1951 / Olivia Casberg.
        p.   cm.
    ISBN 0-933380-07-0
    1. Casberg, Olivia, 1910-   --Childhood and youth. 2. Barrow,
Point (Alaska)--Biography. 3. Barrow, Point (Alaska)--Social life
and customs. 4. Eskimos--Alaska--Barrow, Point.   I. Title.
CT275.C3434A3   1989
979.8'7--dc20
    [B]   89-8644
                                                                  CIP

Olivia Casberg

(805) 688-5036

955 Elk Grove Lane
Solvang, California 93463

Typesetting: Julie Gillies

OLIVE PRESS PUBLICATIONS
P.O. Box 99, Los Olivos, California 93441
(805)688-2445

Printed in the United States of America

TABLE OF CONTENTS

INTRODUCTION

The word, ALASKA, means Great Land. It has an area of 586,400 square miles with 26,300 miles of coast line. Mt. McKinley is 20,300 feet high. The highest peak in North America. Its minerals consist of silver, copper, gold, iron, tin, oil and coal. Unending timber grows there. Fish abound. Animals? Well, there are bear, wolf, muskrat, mink, ermine, lynx, sable, beaver, marmot, hare, squirrel, wolverine, sea and river otter. There are fur seal, walrus and fox. And, we still have a few whales.

Credit is given Sheldon Jackson, for introducing, in the late 1800s, the Siberian reindeer into Alaska.

The deer became food and clothing for the Eskimo and replaced the whale and walrus which, so ruthlessly, for years had been slaughtered.

Over a period of ten years, Dad served the United States Department of Education -   first, in the Nome area and later, in Wainwright - establishing English speaking schools. It was while teaching in Wainwright that Dad was told about a buried village near Barrow. On his return to the States he informed the late John Wanamaker, Sr. about this village.

Mr. Wanamaker was immediately interested. He gave a substantial grant to finance my father's archeological diggings near Barrow.

My Dad. Explorer, Wanderer, Digger, and Mover of both Alaskan tundra and his family in his ten years of explorations.

The turn-of-the-century Alaska was primitive. Few white men ventured that far north. Only traders and explorers. Very few women penetrated that frozen wilderness.

In three years of digging at Barrow, Dad exhumed from the tundra eighty-three prehistoric bodies. Just recently, scientists have carbon dated those bodies as 2,000 years old.

Into this land which my father called "THE TIP TOP OF THE WORLD" he took our family of three.

Revenue cutter "BEAR" took us to Wainwright. She was Admiral Byrd's ship for his first trip to the South Pole

GRUBSTAKING*

A tiny girl pressed her nose against a frost-covered window and said, "Papa, why didn't the sun come up today?" It had been a week since anyone had seen the sun. Why? No clouds. Only dark blue skies. Twilight at noonday. My childish mind couldn't understand.

Philippine crew on the "BEAR"

---

*The Alaskan prospector's term for provisions and outfitting.

War clouds hung low over Europe. How Papa longed to join the American doughboys across the Atlantic. He was too old. Yes, thirty-three was just a little over the age limit for World War One. Here in the far north, he was completely removed from war.

Teaching the Eskimo dance to Olive

But he was carrying on a battle all his own. A battle with the elements. A battle with the centuries-old frozen tundra, where he was in the process of uncovering a prehistoric burial ground.

"To answer your question, Olive dear, this is the land of the midnight sun. For two months in the summer the sun is always with us. But in the winter for two months, our sun hides below the horizon."

Months before, Papa had asked my Mom, "Ethyl, if and when I get a grant to dig for three years will you go North with me again?"

"I should say not. I've had quite enough of that frozen region of the world. Will Van Valin, you know my conditions! Now, since you won't give me what I asked for, all I want to do is stay in my beloved California where I can die of the heat, if I choose to."

It was decided then that Ethyl and their little daughter would stay with grandfather Barnhart and Will, the explorer, would go on alone with his grant for archeological research from the late John Wanamaker. He had great hopes for what he might find at Barrow.

So much to plan for. Everything had to be grubstaked in by boat. Lumber to build a cabin, nails, insulation material, double windows, roofing shingles, chimneys and Chick Sales equipment. All foods except meat for three years, canned or dried. And what was most important, cameras and ten thousand feet of movie film with all materials to do his own developing and printing.

All of Mother's two hundred pounds stood firm as she said, "Good-bye, Will, we will see you in three years. Remember, if you had agreed to give me my request I would have been going along with you."

The train got as far as Seattle, and Will couldn't stand it any longer. Off went the cable: "Can't go on alone. Will grant request. Waiting in Port of Seattle."

I remember the confusion as Mother grubstaked for the two of us. Needles and thread, yarn, yardage of various weights and colors. Oh yes, a rooster and eight hens were included. We had to think of all kinds of things we take so for granted in the States, or the "Outside" as we called the States then. We decided on lightweight tableware, so we bought aluminum flatware, aluminum plates and cups. No plastic or stainless steel then!

"Why didn't you agree to go with Papa in the first place?" I asked as we moved through the aisles of the big department store. "You'll find out soon enough." And mother went on shopping. She proceeded to the baby department of the store and began loading up with diapers, baby undershirts and baby dresses.

Wow, a baby. And in that primitive place? I thought, but didn't say anything.

The "BEAR" guitar group. My first lesson in directing

I had been told that the mail took over six months to reach Barrow. First by train. By ship next. And the last lap of 800 miles, by dog team. There were no radios. No airplanes. What would happen if she needed medical care? My mind was spinning questions I couldn't answer.

One reassuring fact that I had heard was that the Presbyterians had sent a doctor to Pt. Barrow.

Papa was going to give Mother a baby!

The "ARCTIC" which Papa said was "the speediest vessel in the Bering Sea." A fifty-ton schooner with two forty-horsepower motors was chartered by my dad for the last part of our journey to Barrow

IGLOO VAN

The building of a cabin in the Arctic is something quite different than the usual construction job. We took lumber enough for a structure ten feet by twenty feet with a lean-to or shed for storage and the toilet. Insulation which was so very important, was achieved by using two wooden walls with several layers of tar paper in between. We took further precautions against the cold by stuffing the spaces between the two-by-fours with sod from the tundra. Then, when the winter blizzards came, we took great blocks of solid snow and banked them around the house up to the eaves. Double windows were installed, but that didn't prevent an inch of ice forming on the inside windows. Temperatures of fifty and sixty degrees below zero with a wind factor up to 80 degrees below were common!

Freeze-dried clothes on the line. Our drinking water in ice form. The shed housed our toilet

This little cabin served as kitchen, dining room, parlor and bedroom for three. That is tight living. But it was lucky it wasn't any bigger. It took all of Papa's ingenuity to keep the place warm. His stove was purchased in Nome. It was both a heating and cooking coal burner. And never imagining that in a land so full of coal deposits, he wouldn't be able to buy coal, he waited to purchase it at a port beyond Nome. There wasn't any coal. Port after port he tried to buy coal. None! What a frightening thing.

My play tent on the left available when the temperature "warmed" to 35 degrees BELOW

The kitchen of our twenty-foot cabin

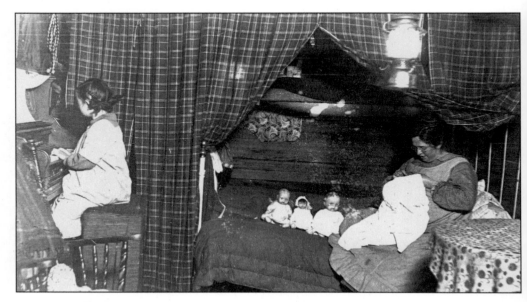

The bedroom end of our cabin. My bunk was on the wall above the double bed, and my first lessons on the organ

He landed in Barrow without coal. There, a friend came to his rescue. Cook Hansen at the local trading post said, "I have some coal dust which I purchased from the Japanese. Maybe that would help?" We kept from freezing that first winter with the use of seal blubber cut in squares, driftwood we picked up along the coast and those precious bags of coal dust. We were many frozen miles from a forest.

There was a 52-gallon water barrel reservoir connected to the stove which supplied us with hot water for washing. But our drinking water was "old" ice melted in another barrel close to the stove. Our old ice was stacked in great blocks near the cabin. It had been brought in from the sea where the salt had been eliminated slowly through seasonal changes.

Seven feet below the surface of the ground we had a room 21 feet in diameter. There, we had our refrigerator system. Shelves around the room were stacked with ducks, geese, whale meat, reindeer, seal, walrus and fish. We sampled meat that was several years old and it was still as fresh as when it was first put in. Meat was our main dish. No fresh vegetables or fruits were available. We lived on dried potatoes, dried eggs and canned milk. Our butter

Our underground permafrost freezer with ducks, deer, seal and walrus

came in big barrels of salt water. I never knew about vitamins until I was in my twenties. But no vitamin deficiency was apparent. The meat, eaten raw or cooked, seemed to provide what we needed to keep healthy. Neither my brother nor I had scurvy, rickets or bowed legs.

Papa built a box which hung outside the window for our ice cream. He used to make several freezers full and store them in this window refrigerator. I still remember the wonderful aroma of that ice cream box when he reached in to get our dessert for the evening. He would build up a hot fire in the stove and open the oven door. Then, he pulled up our chairs and we would stick our feet in the oven and eat ice cream as we listened to the blizzard whine around the eaves of our cozy cabin.

The lean-to built against the house measured six by ten. It provided an entrance way as well as a corner for our one-seater "Chick Sales." There we hung a curtain which provided privacy against visitors who might be offended by sight or smell. Freezing it always was, out there! No wonder then that we had frequent episodes of constipation. Mother's great remedy was castor oil. "Now, Olive, swallow it", and she stuck that tablespoon of evil smelling stuff in my mouth. I used to gag and she threatened me, "I'll just give you more if you vomit it. If you swallow it properly I will give you a stick of gum." I would have swallowed anything for that precious stick of gum. That was such a luxury in Alaska at that time. But the association of peppermint and castor oil became so common that for 30 years afterward I still tasted castor oil when I tasted peppermint, be it in the form of candy, gum or drink.

The Eskimo had no toilets then. Women pulled their parkas about them in a circle and squatted on the snow. The men with their handy gadgets used a snow bank nearby. So, there were yellow circles with an occasional brown spot all over the winter snows until the next snowfall would bury the colors.

One day, as we were about to complete our one-room masterpiece, old friend, Kotuk, knocked at our door and asked if he might come and have a look. He was dressed in the usual reindeer ateegee (coat), seal skin kumicks (boots), and fur pants. Kotuk was considered a "big" man in the village. His wife had sewn his clothes with great care. Lots of pretty fur patterns, plus a ruffle of wolverine fur edging his coat. Kotuk looked about the place with interest. He admired the double windows. He was impressed with our method of insulation and loved our petromax lantern. Petromaxes were used because there was no electricity. This kerosene lamp with a little pump in its side and its little white wick made it seem almost as bright as an electric light. But, as Kotuk looked at the ceiling, he commented, "He no nose." We weren't sure what he meant. So, he explained that every building in this

An Eskimo snow covered winter home with translucent ice-block entrance

climate had to be ventilated so as to get rid of the condensation created by heat inside against the severe cold outside. Much to our dismay at losing hot air up that vent, we put the hole right through the ceiling and roof. It did prove to be helpful in reducing the formation of ice on the inside windows and under the bed.

This was our home for two and a half years. I had my first music lessons on an old pump organ which we had scrounged from Grandmother Barnhart's antiques. We figured we would rather cut into the freight allowance for food than to be without music for the years ahead. Mother taught me how to crochet. I made granny squares by the dozens. Mother wouldn't allow me to attend the local Eskimo school because she hated the white government teacher. So, she took on the task of teaching me to read and write. Papa was gone a great deal of the time. Even in the dark months he supervised the diggings on the beach near Barrow.

Twice before, Papa had had tours of Alaskan duty under the U.S. Board of Education. During that time, he was made aware of a buried village at Barrow. The Eskimo loved and trusted him. He was not only teacher of their children, he was their dentist, doctor and in charge of the town's reindeer industry. He really wasn't a doctor, but I remember seeing him take down the great big book of medicine and study about the most recent case of sickness he had on his hands. He never lost a patient, even though some came awfully close to death. Kotuk fell ill after his visit with us. And Papa writes in his diary about his serious bout with death, "While hunting seal one day my friend injured his finger on a rusty wire. Blood poison set in. A runner came to the cabin and asked for medicine. 'Kotuk is very sick, Mr. Van Valin. I'm afraid he will die'." Papa sent some medicine. In two weeks word came again, "Kotuk is worse." The messenger was troubled, "Mr. Van, red streaks are going up his arms now. He is in great pain. He has lost many pounds."

"You must bring him here," Papa said. "I will take care of him myself."

"He will not come, Sir. He is afraid that the bumps on the ice will hurt him too much." And the messenger turned away.

Finally, Kotuk was forced to come with his trusty dog team. In the school house Papa made him a bed on the floor and began to treat him. He gave him morphine first to ease his pain. He gave him strychnine for his heart. And then, he prepared hot flaxseed poultices for his hand until the skin broke and a great deal of green pus was released. Papa's diary records, "The swelling subsided, but we couldn't save the finger. We cut it off. The bone in it was like a sponge. That old medical book which I brought to Alaska with me worked again!" He had saved Kotuk's life.

Papa was judge of the town when the Eskimos couldn't settle their own problems. He went with them on their whaling expeditions. He fished and hunted with them and several times he almost lost his life at sea. At home, Papa was our baker. Once a week, out would come the sourdough starter (yeast), the sack of flour and the dish

What is left of Igloo Van c1984

pan. Out of that kneaded mess would come the finest tasting bread ever made. From that batch, he would set aside another sourdough starter for the following week.

And so, our family of three settled into a primitive cabin measuring ten-by-twenty feet. And for three long years we lived hundreds of miles above the Arctic Circle where they had never heard of radio, a television or an airplane.

MOTHER

My childhood remembrances of Mother were not pleasant. She was unforgiving, nervous, loud-voiced and critical. She often taunted my Papa. Her tirades began in a high-pitched, "Will Van Valin!" She loved her father, and wished out loud so many times that Will would "only be like my father."

Mother Van and Olive -- renamed by her Eskimo friends, Petungnak (Fair Wind) at age two -- 1912

Memories of her outbursts when I was with her alone were frightening for a young child. "I have an awful headache. I think I am going to die," she threatened, and I'd run and hide in the closet. The frequent threats of her dying gave me nightmares. Then, she would complain to me about Papa and how he didn't make a decent living. "You will never know what I have gone through," she repeated so

Mother in Eskimo ateegee (coat)

many times that it became a cliché. I used to wonder if she was deliberately trying to make me hate my father.

There was an attic in our first Alaskan home near Nome. A chimney from the coal stove below warmed a little sandpile in the corner of the upper floor. When things became too tense, I would steal up the ladder, sit by my sandpile and let the tiny, soft, clean grains slip through my fingers. Tension and ugly thoughts slipped away like the sand.

Papa had tried many times to teach me how to whistle, but I didn't do it quite right. One morning in my attic, I pursed my lips and out came a whistle. Whistling by my sandpile was the therapy I needed in those early years. And even now as the tensions of life disturb my peace, whistling is good medicine.

Papa had his way of silencing Mother's outbursts. I never heard him answer back. But he would reach for his guitar and sit in our one rocker and sing until she quieted down. It's hard to scream at someone with pretty music in the room. I don't remember Mother ever saying, "I'm sorry," or "I was wrong." I learned very young to take a negative stance to most of her positions. If she began yelling, I got quiet. If she criticized, I tried to see the good. If she tried to defend me among playmates, I said "Mother, please let me fight my own battles." Hers was a world battling against people and things. Always judgmental. Never forgetting an injustice done her. And completely self-centered. Mother had been raised in a very religious family. Both her parents were ministers. Why, oh why, I wondered as the years went by. Why weren't the truths taught in that strict home, more evident in my mother's life?

She and I had many hours alone in our wilderness home when Papa was on the beach with his Eskimo diggers. "You know," she would moan, "I could have been the

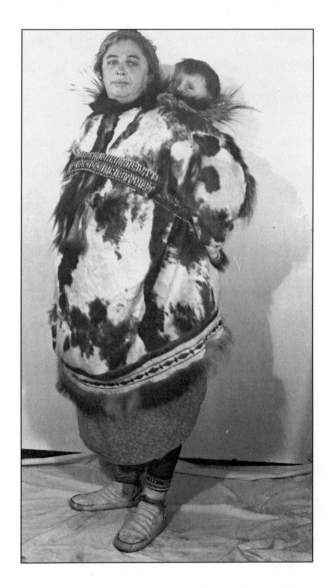

Mother demonstrating the Eskimo backpack

leading soprano in Pittsburg." She never let me forget her frustrated dream and her sorrow for making the decision to marry and go West.

Beneath the quiet exterior of her lover, lay something she didn't discover until later. He harbored a call to the wild.

Papa and Olive at Sinuk, May 1913. Note Olive's gun

He couldn't tame it. "A homestead in Washington," he promised. "Acres and acres just waiting for the two of us." It turned out to be bear country.

Now, what was happening to her dream of becoming a musician? I think, early on, she felt her unfulfilled dreams might be realized in me. She set me up to a little pump organ and taught me my notes. And maybe, I have thought many times since, maybe, because I didn't follow through and become her prima donna, maybe that was the reason she didn't love me.

In Alaska she became a mountain of fat. Three hundred pounds we guessed, but no bathroom scales ever disclosed her secret. Her appearance could certainly have been forgiven if she had developed a loving, forgiving personality. She was a matriarch in the real sense of the word. She tried to dominate everyone around her.

I tried many times through the years to make peace with

Mother. I did her hair. I sewed her clothes. I tried, very diplomatically, to counsel her regarding her attitudes toward people. "You just don't understand. You will never understand!" she complained, and I finally gave up.

I learned early in life NEVER to be obligated to her. There was one attribute which she developed to perfection as she grew older. Favors given were SURE to require something in return. I can still hear, "All I have done for you and this is the way you treat me!" She never forgave her son-in-law, Mel, who took her to task when she was trying to break up her son's marriage. She held it against Mel for the rest of her life, even though he took on her complete medical care until she died.

"Why can't you be happy, Mother?" My exasperation at times turned into impatience, "You have no REAL tragedies in your life. Your two children have not disgraced you nor have they given you heartaches."

Our family with Kudlook, a government apprentice

Repeatedly through the years, I tried to beautify her surroundings. Once, returning from India, I found her in a cluttered little apartment. My experience in designing and redecorating homes gave me confidence that I could create a little paradise in which she could spend her waning years. "Mother," I pled, "let me clean up the place. Let me redecorate it. Let me clean out the pots and pans you never use anymore." Trunks full of old furs from her Alaskan days cluttered the storage areas. She had art and attractive objects from her years of travel, but they lay hidden in the confusion of junk which she had accumulated. A garage full of Alaskan curios and artifacts harbored black widow spiders and thousands of moths.

But, she wouldn't let me help her.

She preferred to wheel about through the dust and debris, the dirty little bathroom and the unsightly kitchen.

I have seen this domineering female all but destroy a man. And from my babyhood days she used to say, "You keep nothing from your mother. You must tell me everything." This was the rule of my life until I left home for college. And when I said, "Yes" to my future husband before I had consulted her, my conscience gave me fits. From her perch in the wheel chair, she spoke with such authority that the faint of heart could scarcely question let alone contradict her "majesty."

During my India years, I was far away enough to try and forget what she was really like. I used to dream of the Mother I wanted her to be. And in those years my dreams almost made her over. I wanted to respect her. I longed for mother love.

Then, I would come back to California with high expectations only to be dismayed with my findings. I am now far enough removed from the person I knew, to look back objectively and forgivingly, yet realistically. She gave me life. She fed me. And clothed me. And I am grateful.

But what an enigma she was.

What a contradiction in values. Never have I met another human being like my Mother. She was a "stranger-than-fiction character." She was masterful in the art of hiding from the public her negative attributes.

Through the waning years of her marriage, as if it were retribution of a kind, she was forced into caring for an invalid husband. Perhaps, this was the "prison" she deserved.

Now, this was the person who went to share the life of my everlastingly-patient Papa in Point Barrow, Alaska.

MY FIRST LOVE

The aurora borealis, with colors like a rainbow, dipped and swayed as waves on a black sea. They playfully encircled the steeple of the little white chapel at Barrow as we mushed by.

I was to be a guest at the Trading Post which was owned and managed by Charlie Brower.

Mother Brower, Charlie's Eskimo wife, offered to have me join her four children in their attic bedroom. "Bring your sleeping bag, Petungnak, and wear your warmest ateegee (coat)."

Over the icy tundra my big collie raced the little sled. There was a lot of excitement among the children that night. The little white girl was coming. "You know," they whispered among themselves, "her Mom is having a baby."

David was one of Mother Brower's four. I had watched him many times at a distance as he played with the boys. He was sort of special somehow. And tonight I was going to David's house! David did single me out that night. Did he guess how flattered I was? He took me through his father's Trading Post with its shelves laden with goodies. Lots of fur skins which the Eskimo had traded in for tea and sugar. There was gum and hard candy. Wow, I hadn't seen any gum for months. He slipped me some. He said, "Petungnak, you know my father is a white man. I guess that's why I like you. You smell good. People tell me that you're a lot whiter than we are because you bathe too much."

I laughed. For we had no proper bathroom and it was rare that I bathed more than once a week and THAT -- in an old galvanized tub in our one-room cabin by the big stove.

David went on, "Do you like me, even though I'm half Eskimo? I have a good body. I manage a gun even though I'm only ten. My dad has a lot of money. You know, he may own those lakes of oil east of Barrow some day."

I was impressed.

"Some day, my Dad may send me 'Outside'. I can go to school there and learn a lot."

The dinner bell rang. What a dinner it was! David had ordered a special treat. Actually, had helped the cook crank some homemade chocolate ice cream. After dinner of reindeer roast, dried potatoes and freshly baked sourdough bread, David and I walked under the aurora borealis.

"Could I come and see you sometime in your snow tent?" Because of the intense Arctic cold, my parents had pitched a play tent close to our cabin. David went on shyly, "We could play together and rub noses. Do you have cooties like most of us? Oh, probably not. It wouldn't hurt you to have a few anyway."

The aurora borealis dipped and swayed above us. "Time for bed," Mother Brower called, and rang the night bell. Children took to the attic and sleeping bags.

I must add a postlude.

"Look Mel," (now my husband of 57 years) "look quick. There's David Brower from Alaska." David, my first love, flashed across the TV screen in a news item about the large Alaskan earthquake!

Tommy Brower, David's brother, now lives in Barrow. He is a prosperous businessman who has played an important and influential role in the development of the North Slope Borough.

LAKES OF OIL and
THE FIRST WHITE CHILD BORN
AT POINT BARROW

More and more talk of oil on the tundras east of us intrigued the white men of Barrow. So Papa and the local school teacher decided to do some exploring.

William B. Van Valin--the first white man to stake out these lakes of oil east of Barrow

Several days passed. Then, the sound of the dog teams heralded their return, and not any too soon. Baby was due any moment. Papa burst into the cabin with, "Ethyl, I have found the most fantastic thing. I actually saw large lakes of crude oil! Acres of that black stuff on the surface of the ground. I staked them out. I suppose it is foolish to think it could ever be delivered to the States. Nevertheless, I staked 'em."

Most northerly Eskimo home on continental North America

My family standing next to igloo on the most northern point of land in Alaska. Eskimos call it "Nuvuk" which means "point". We are dressed in reindeer clothing with cotton "ategrelooks" or cloth covers to keep the snow out of the fur. It is April and very cold

Kuk River coal mine which Papa discovered. This coal burns with very little ash

Mother, now great with child, couldn't be less interested. It was cold in the cabin. There was ice under the bed. Our blankets froze to the walls. She was afraid the canned milk would freeze on the shelves. The precious cans might burst. She finally responded with, "It will be a miracle if you ever realize anything from your find."

"Will Van Valin, it's time you were chipping out the ice from under my bed. The child is about to be born. Olive's gone to Charlie Brower's place. She's been invited to bunk with his children until I am through with this ordeal. Oil or no oil, let's get on with the preparations for the new baby."

The delivery of that first white child born at Barrow was complicated. The baby had to be rotated in utero. Dr. Spense, the Presbyterian missionary, had no instruments.

Baby-sitting my brother, Bill

Olive with Eskimo baby climbing steps out of a snow house

49

And I've heard Mother say, "If he hadn't had small hands, the delivery would have ended in tragedy."

That baby boy, lived to become a doctor in the little Danish village of Solvang, California.

Papa's name goes on.

Adrift on an iceberg near Barrow with my screaming baby brother

REINDEER ROUNDUP TIME

We had no fences at Point Barrow. There were no trees to chop down. So, when roundup time came, the men cut huge blocks of ice and frozen snow to build a corral.

Papa invited me to go with him to see the great herds of reindeer. It was a bright, sunny day and the snow sparkled like a million diamonds. It was beautiful. But soon, my eyes felt like I was going blind. I spoke to Papa, "Something is wrong with my eyes, I can't see very well."

Reindeer roundup, c1916

Papa understood. He had had the same experience many times. "I'll find you some dark glasses right away."

Snow blindness is rather common in that part of the world when bright sunlight is mirrored on the snow. And before dark glasses were available, the old Eskimo had carved wooden blinders with slits which ran the width of the face.

Hundreds of reindeer were brought in that day by the herders from the tundras east and south of Barrow. Each animal had to be felled and branded with its proper owner's initials. My remembrance of the food that day is vivid. Never had I been allowed to drink tea at home. But

Reindeer roundup--Eskimo "cowboys" with sled deer

I was SO cold! Besides, my Mother wasn't there. Men, you know, are a "soft touch" with little girls, so I got my tea — twelve ounces of it in a big tin jug.

I watched the men butcher deer for the winter supply of the villagers. One group of men caught my eye. They were enjoying something to eat out of the open belly of the deer. They were dipping out a green substance from the stomach of the animal and were actually eating it and

Cutting ownership marks on the ears of a reindeer fawn, June 1915

enjoying it. "Won't you have some, Petungnak? It's sweet like candy." Well, I thought, frozen whale skin with blubber is good. Maybe this green stuff might be all right. It was sweet as they had said, but I really never learned to like it.

In 1939 President Roosevelt signed a bill which authorized the purchase of all the reindeer owned by the white man. This put the industry in the hands of the Eskimo. It is hard to think how they could have survived these many years without these animals. Their warmest clothing is made from its hides. Skins from the legs of two reindeer make the uppers for their kumiks, or boots. The deer meat is sweet and juicy and very tender. The blood is frozen and used in soups and dog food. The marrow from the bones is boiled and used with salmon berries, tomcod liver and seal oil to make what they call "Eskimo ice cream". The sinew from their backs makes the Eskimo's strongest thread.

Knife handles, dog harnesses, swivels and bows for archers are made from the horns.

It is difficult to milk a deer. So, they lay them on the ground. It was reported to us one day that the mouth of the milker became the milking machine, squirting it then into a container. The very container we were using on our table. It took two or three deer to make a quart of milk.

This domesticated reindeer is relinquishing its milk under protest. Sometimes, to keep fingers from freezing, the Eskimos extract the milk into their mouths and then spit into a bottle

We had been enjoying our "fresh" milk until we heard about their method of milking. Papa decided, then, that our dried milk was more to his liking, and decidedly better for our health. At that time, tuberculosis was common among the residents of Barrow.

In Papa's diary, he tells of the way the deer used their horns. "They don't fight with them as often as we might guess. Instead, they charge and fight with their front hoofs. If the horns were really for the purpose of offense or defense, the deer would be unprotected for several months out of the year. They shed them each season in the spring. The velvet, when shed, hangs in great strands from the horns. Then, it is said that the deer eat their horns when they drop. This may be a way of replacing the calcium they need to grow new ones.

"The food of the deer in that part of Alaska consists of grass, a small ground willow and a pale green lichen called reindeer moss. There are dead willow leaves in this food, and they do a remarkable job of separating the dead from the vegetation. As they chew, one may observe the dried material dropping from the corners of their mouths."

The ability of these animals to endure Arctic blizzards is miraculous. They have no barns or shelters of any kind. And when the mercury shows 60 degrees below zero, they head into the storm, dig through the snow with their spatulate, concave hoofs and pick the moss out before the snow refills the hole again.

Reindeer may be trained to be used as a sled deer. But they do not travel as fast nor have the endurance of dogs. When they are being trained they may be vicious. Standing on their hind legs they can strike terrific blows at the trainer. Sometimes, when harnessed to the sled, they are given to dashing off like a shot, leaving the driver lunging for the sled or dragging behind it. There are, however, sled deer who can be trained to be very gentle.

Mother and I took one of those gentle creatures on a long, long, trip for that part of the world -- ninety frozen miles. I was only 7 years old, but I spelled Mother off when she got tired driving.

The Eskimo have Sheldon Jackson to thank for introducing the reindeer into the far north. It was his dream to bring them from Siberia. The U.S. Government said no at first. He then turned to private donors. Their initial investment was 16 reindeer. They did so well on the meager food from the tundras, and multiplied so rapidly, that the Government appropriated $5,000 to buy more deer.

From this nucleus, a great industry has developed. An industry which has fed and clothed the Eskimo for almost a century.

NINETY MILES BY SLED DEER FROM WAINWRIGHT TO BARROW

"Olive, your mother and I have to take a long journey through the snow and across ice fields tomorrow. I'll be driving the dog team but I've arranged for you and Ethyl to drive a sled deer. It's a mild-natured animal, and I'm sure you will be safe following my team. Your mother will no doubt get tired and I wish you would spell her off when she does. Remember, sled deer are handled differently than horses. Instead of two reins, a reindeer is controlled by one. You flip it over the right side for a right turn, and to the left when you want to go left. It's really simple."

The animal proved to be gentle. We amateur drivers did okay. There were no villages along the way. No motels. Just vast snow-covered miles without trees or hills. But we didn't try to make the trip in one day. Ninety miles by sled deer can be very tiring.

Mother and Olive enroute from Wainwright to Barrow-- a ninety-mile trip via single rein sled deer, June 1915

Our Eskimo guide said we must stop early so he and his helpers could construct a snow house. The men began to chop and cut out great blocks of snow. Frozen snow can

My favorite sled deer with a magnificent rack in velvet

be as hard as ice. They soon had about a dozen large blocks. These they stacked so as to form a rounded snow igloo (house).

We unloaded our fur blankets, laid them out on the snow floor, lit a little kerosene lamp and brought out the dinner. Did you ever taste frozen kidney beans? We had them for dinner that night along with frozen hard tack. They called it, "pilot bread." And really, it all tasted very good, for I was awfully hungry.

Snow houses can be used for only a couple days. The heat from our bodies and breath begins to melt the snow. Ice then forms on ceiling and sides making the temperature unbearably cold. We built only one snow house on the way, for by the end of the next day we had reached our destination at the Barrow Trading Post.

Eskimo freight service hauling wood

SPELL OF THE YUKON

On one of Papa's trips into Alaska he became aware of a strange affliction which victimized many a gold-rush man. Good friends starting out together on this great adventure to the northland found it difficult to adjust to many of the hardships. The cold. The isolation. The hunger and just the tedium of life.

They began to get on each other's nerves and they would quarrel over the most trivial matters. Too often, men didn't return from the Yukon. For that reason, before they were permitted to go into the wilderness areas, mounted police were careful to register everyone. Name. Where they had come from. Height. Weight. Color of eyes and hair. And especially what weapon they were carrying.

Guns were sometimes taken and stored for their owners until their return.

A story is told by a Miss Walton, an unusual woman of the North. She was mushing down the Kobuk River with her dog team, through deep snow the day before Christmas when all of a sudden her dogs stopped in their tracks, put up their noses, and headed off through the timber to a lonely log cabin. Miss Walton was curious, so she let the dogs go. She went up to the door and knocked. To her surprise, a tall, handsome, bearded prospector answered and invited her in. He wasn't alone. The other man said, "Woman, where under God's heaven did YOU come from? Come over here by the stove and thaw out. You must be nearly frozen." Immediately, Miss Walton felt the tension in the room. It was obvious the men weren't speaking to each other. There seemed to be an invisible division in the cabin. Each one had placed his belongings in a different corner.

Sensing the disagreement and recognizing it for what it was, she stepped to the center of the room and drew a straight line from wall to wall, "Now gentleman, this is Christmas week. We're all a long way from home. I am going to cook a nice dinner at my place tomorrow. But I'm not going to invite either of you until you step to this center line and shake hands." The men looked at each other and then, like little boys with a smile of chagrin, shook hands.

"We'll be there tomorrow, Miss Walton." And the spell of the Yukon was broken. "We were ready to kill each other when you came in Miss Walton. We'll take your offer of a good dinner now. Merry Christmas!"

Papa ran into another situation on the Yukon River one day. This time several men were involved. A big German had drawn a knife on his fellow crewmen as they paddled down the river. A Swedish sailor and his brother, seeing the situation, pulled alongside the feuding crewmen and yelled, "Hey, you numskulls. What's going on? Put away that knife." He turned to the crewmen and challenged, "I dare you to take on this German, one by one."

They knew that not one of them was a match for the German, so they agreed to pull ashore and settle their differences in the proper way. The big Swede agreed to act as their arbitrator.

And again, the spell of the Yukon was broken.

But this kind of situation was common among the men who followed the unlikely and unpromising trail to gold in the Arctic.

POLAR BEAR HUNTING

What an unusually crafty hunter the old-time Eskimo was. When one has no gun he has to be creative. The way he caught the polar bear in those early years, was absolutely ingenious. He would make blubber or fat balls by winding strips of whale bone sharpened at the ends with slices of fat. Round and round, he would wind the fat with the whale bone until he had a ball about the size of a baseball. He then would tie it with some sinew string and lay it out on the ice to freeze. When it was frozen hard, he would take off the string and place the ball on the ice ready for his prey.

When a bear swallows the fat ball it takes only a short time to melt and cause the points on the whale bone to spring loose. At this point they begin to pierce the walls of the bear's stomach.

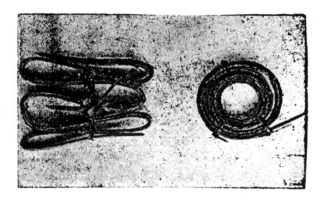

Eskimo polar bear death pills

The hunter watches from a safe distance and when the bear begins to roll in agony and tries to vomit, turns somersaults and dives into the icy water, the hunter knows it won't be long before the bear will have spent his strength. At this point the hunter can move in and spear him. He now has a month's supply of food for his family without having fired a shot.

A bear in a losing fight with a death pill

This seems like a cruel way to kill, but the Eskimo argue that the bear is a great robber. "He steals from the villagers' caches, the food which is important to the survival of our people through the long winter. He's a sneaky hunter too." And they go on to tell the story of the bears' tricks.

They have observed him lying motionless at a seal blow hole, covering his black nose with his paws so as not to be seen by the seal when he comes up for air. The bear will leap on him and crush his head between his powerful jaws. The bear is choosy about his diet and eats only the blubber and skin, leaving the rest of the meat and bones for the wise fox who has learned to follow the hunter-bear. The Eskimo swear they have seen bear jump from the ice onto the back of a passing whale and bite out great mouthfuls of whale skin and fat. He has been known to kill a sleeping walrus by breaking its neck with a large cake of ice.

Now, these were the Eskimo's stories told to my father in the early 1900s. Perhaps, it was their attempt to justify their own hunting practices.

ARCTIC HUNTING STORIES

Hunting was always hazardous in the Arctic. The following are a few of Papa's experiences at sea. He calls this one

Trapped Among Flowers of Ice

One of my most thrilling and serious experiences occurred on a late fall day when I went to sea to get some fresh meat. Unlashing my small oomiak (open Eskimo skin boat) from its cache and slipping my .22 high-power Savage rifle in the bow, I pushed off the beach. Looking over the side, I could see through the transparent water, large florescent ice crystals forming on the gravel and stones on the bottom of the sea.

"Curious," I thought. I had never noticed them before, nor could I understand the cause of their formation now, especially before the surface had frozen over. I noticed several of them breaking loose and floating to the surface. Some singly and some in clusters. They came bobbing up like corks.

I spotted an ugaruk (bearded seal) some distance out and started toward it. He ducked before I could take aim. So I rowed on, following him until I was about a mile from shore.

I noticed those ice flowers beginning to join together, like pancakes, about a foot in diameter. I found it difficult rowing through them. Then, the pancakes started to join up forming an icy scum.

THE AIR TURNED COLD VERY SUDDENLY!

I was frightened. It became more and more difficult to row through that scum.

"Guess I'd better head for shore," I said to myself out loud.

The young ice formed so rapidly that the oars had to be raised high and dropped with force to get a hold in the thickening mush. I was afraid to force the boat too severely against the ice, for the edges were knife-like and threatened the skin of the oomiak.

I was in a lather of perspiration. Not so much from the exertion but from the mental strain and anxiety. I felt I was being paralyzed, little by little. My knees and hands were numb with cold. My arms ached from hard rowing against the wind which was carrying me farther out to sea.

"I'm surely a prisoner of this storm. My chances of surviving are poorer every passing minute. Oh, God help!"

I knew I would freeze to death in the boat before the ice would be sufficiently strong to bear my weight.

Suddenly, my boat seemed to glide ahead with much less pull. I had found an open lead in the ice left by some native hunter who had passed through just a few minutes earlier. He knew the way home better than I. This course led me directly into the current of the Sinuk River, and I was safe. That shore never looked so good.

The Seal Hunt

One beautiful, clear, calm morning in the month of April, Papa writes, I decided to hunt seal off the shore. I would have to go three miles out.

The sea was a mirror. Perfectly placid. A half hour's rowing through this spell-binding environment and I landed on the edge of the floe ice. I pulled my oomiak out on the ice and sat down to watch for game.

A young leopard seal stuck his head up within range. A shot from my trusty gun and my floating hook brought it out on the ice beside me. I was about to put it in the boat when I glanced up the coast and saw evidence of the wind breaking through the Sawtooth Range at Tissue River about 25 miles away. It was a warning, I was sure.

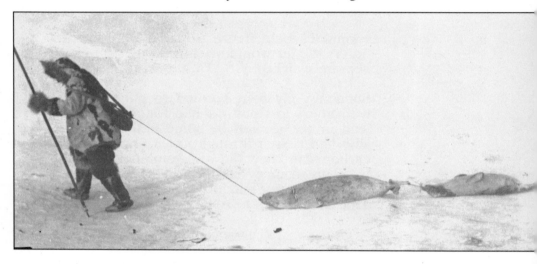

Successful seal hunt--seals are normally taken at a blow hole .

Another hunter, Isuk, had just arrived to join me. "Tow tuk pein, anoe azeruk! Eluktoonga," I said in my whaler's poor Eskimo. (Look you, plenty bad wind. I am going.)

"Nanacoon, woong ah", he replied. (I will come by and by.)

I hadn't cleared the slack ice before a tempestuous wind struck, and the white caps were breaking all around me. The sea became short and choppy. A swell would rise, and a wooly would snap the tops off and cover me with spray. Deep into the valley between two liquid mountains I would slide, and then rise again on their rolling backbones. The swells had to be ridden just right, or I would capsize into the trough of the sea.

My only concern at this point was to keep afloat.

When at last, I reached the beach, I looked out over the waves to see what had become of my friend, Isuk. At times, I would catch sight of him on the crest of a big wave. Then, he would disappear as though he had been swamped. Then, he would appear again. He had tied his gut ateegee (rain coat made of seal intestines) around the hoop of his kyak, and although the sea would break over him, the coat kept his kyak from filling with water. I had a lot of respect for this great seaman. I shall always remember the grim determination on his face as he approached the shore. He squeezed his small craft between those great beached icebergs and stepped ashore – SOAKED IN ICE WATER BUT SAFE AT LAST!

Another hunting story Papa liked to tell was of a young duck hunter, Mungnuk, by name.

He went to sea with us one day to hunt. A flock of eider ducks came by and he took a shot at them. His gun kicked so violently that it capsized his small boat and he went headlong into the frigid water.

He came up. But his head was inside the opening in his upside-down kyak. Lucky for him that it was, for if he had surfaced in the usual way, he would have drowned, for not one Eskimo in a thousand can swim.

He actually climbed inside the skin boat from underneath the water and the air, trapped inside the kayak kept him alive until our crewmen could reach him and pull him to safety.

Except for the loss of his ammunition, shotgun and ducks, he was none the worse.

A young hunter he was, learning the secrets of becoming a good hunter in the unfriendly Arctic.

Eskimo woman butchering a walrus with kayak in back

WHALING AT THE TOP OF THE WORLD

SPRING! It was a time for the men of the village to hitch up the dogs and leave for the open leads of the old ice. Their stay at sea was always uncertain so their sleds were loaded with supplies. We who were left behind watched the horizon, day after day, for a flag which would give the good news that the whalers had made their catch. When the flag appeared the women would gather the children and old folk, hitch up the dog teams for the 20-mile ride, and head for their duties at sea. They would be helping with the butchering and cooking for a big crowd.

The trip out was rough. There were no roads. High ice pressure ridges had to be crossed, and many times a road

"Leaving the village for the twenty-mile trip to the sea where the men had caught the whale"

had to be cut through them. But no one complained. It was a happy trip, for their supply of meat was assured for another season.

The kill was cut and divided carefully between families. It seemed they knew how to be fair to everyone. The Eskimo we knew at that time were a gentle people and very generous. I have often heard my father say, "They would

One-hundred-foot pressure ridge, May 1915

share their last crust with me." A big pile of the meat was stacked for the feast at sea. What a picnic it was!

We didn't dare hazard the miles home in the dark, so after the dogs were fed and the sleds loaded, the women and children were off to shore and home.

No limit was put on the number of whales the Eskimo were allowed to kill in those days, for when the villagers had enough for winter, they stopped killing.

Papa's whaling crew watching and listening for a bowhead blow

Papa and Olive climb over a pressure ridge twenty miles at sea while hunting

Villagers arriving after a successful whaling trip

At the end of the whaling season elaborate celebrations were planned. There was great feasting and lots of games. One of the most interesting games was called Nelakatuk. It was like our trampoline. People gather around a huge round skin made with hides sewn together, and bounce the jumpers into the air. As long as one could remain on his feet he could be tossed up indefinitely. But there were all sorts of tricks to unbalance the fellow on the skin. When

he would fall, it was time for another to take his place.
This went on for hours.

Nelakatuk

"Petungnak" (Olive) takes a turn at jumping on the big skin

During these feast days I was allowed to eat uncooked, frozen whale skin. A half inch of blubber was left on a two-inch thick skin to give it a little extra flavor. I learned to love it and asked for it often. It became my favorite Eskimo food. And frozen. Not cooked. They would hand me a piece about five inches square and an Eskimo fan-shaped knife, and show me how to cut off a bite using this funny knife without cutting my nose or lips. "Doesn't it

83

taste like beechnuts?" said Papa munching on his chunk of black whale skin. "That blubber is actually sweet and not a bit fishy, as so many think."

Eating muktuk with Petungnak and Papa in foreground

Eskimo variation of teeter-totter

Hide-n-seek. One hides and everyone looks for him/her. Hiding places were at a premium on this treeless beach

PAPA'S VIEW OF WHALING

My little girl remembrance of whaling season was quite different from Papa's. For he was the hunter. He writes:

> The season for whales usually began in early spring. One day in May several men already at sea, sighted a whale spouting. All of the crews, including four oomiaks (boats) and ten oomeras (whale boats), began the chase.

> We bombed it twice, but the bombs didn't explode. A harpoon, however, had been implanted so that the crews could follow him. The hunters spread out over an area of two miles, watching and waiting for the next time the whale would surface, for every 20 minutes a whale must come up for air.

> It took two more bombs to finally kill the whale. And, what a sight it was to see fourteen boats, all sails set and filled with a strong wind, rowing this tremendous animal to the edge of the shore ice.

> It was time for the flag. Up to the highest point on the ridge it went. The villagers saw it and knew the whaling crews had been successful.

> A trail then from the floating whale to the solid ice had to be cut. "A dead man" was made in the ice fifty feet back to which double blocks and tackles were made fast. The end of the line was hitched to the whale's luke or tail. By this time, the dog teams began to arrive from the village and 100 Eskimos heaved on the line and brought the whale to its butchering place.

Great squares of skin and blubber were cut out and
placed in a general heap waiting for distribution
among the crews who were on the hunt. The meat
pieces were then cut and divided in the same
fashion. Even the old folks who couldn't make it
out to the kill, waited along the trail home and each
one got a share of the meat and blubber. Through
the years the Eskimo had learned that sharing was
the best policy.

This particular area of the sea seemed to the
hunters to be a good whaling post, so they stashed
their gear and decided to rest for the night. I
spread a canvas on the ice and in my full fur outfit
lay down to sleep.

But I was rudely awakened very suddenly by a
jarring of the ice under me. It was actually moving!
The wind and currents were getting active. I got up
and found Ivuk on sentinel duty. "I don't like the
looks of that moving pressure ridge, Ivuk, don't you
think we ought to get moving towards shore?"

Ivuk took a look through my binoculars. That was
all he needed. All hell broke loose in camp. The
sleeping crew threw whaling gear and food into the
boats on the sleds. The ice began to buckle and
shelve beneath us. We watched it pile up in a big
"windrow" about a hundred yards ahead. It closed
in on our trail.

We were sure by now that we were cut off from
shore. The shaking ice came in from behind us.
From in front of us.
And to our sides.
Crushing.
Pitching.
Rolling and assuming gigantic proportions.

An invisible, screaming, roaring force was splitting, smashing and upheaving ice as high as a two-story building. The ice over which we were racing broke with tremendous pressure and shelved underneath us.

It seemed like a living thing trying to catch us and grind us to bits. Imagine a gigantic plowshare, driven by a million horsepower motor, cleaving the ice and throwing the shattered fragments in every direction.

At this point we were exhausted and our lungs were about to be frostbitten with the deep breathing of the ice wind. I am sure no power on earth could have stopped such a monstrous oncoming pressure ridge. I wished I could have had my camera. But had I stopped one moment to film it, neither cameraman nor picture would ever have been seen again.

Finally, we outran this life-threatening holocaust and pitched another camp along the edge of the shore ice. And, just as it so often happens in the Arctic, the very next day, radiant sunshine fell on the sea and it became as calm as a mill pond.

We bombed another whale not far from our second camp. But before we could harpoon it, the whale went under the ice. The crew kept watch for 24 hours hoping it would surface again. But it was gone!

An old Eskimo with us that day had a reputation of being able to spot a whale under ice, much the same way an oil finder uses a divining rod, or one who uses a stick to find underground water to sink a well.

We went to work. He warned the crew that it might take him several days, for he knew it would take three days at least for a whale to get full of gas and float to the undersurface of the ice. The old man paced back and forth, up and down, zigzagging here and there, hour after hour leaning forward and examining the surface of the ice very carefully. He stopped only to eat and to sleep briefly, for at this time of the year the sun was with us almost constantly.

Sure enough. On the third day a call rang out. "Ahavik monie!" (the whale is here).

I didn't believe him. "Now, my good friend, HOW can you possibly be sure the whale is there?" The young whalers had more confidence in the old man and they began to dig through several feet of ice. Down and down they chipped away. Five feet. Ten feet. "Do you think we should go further?" I asked. And they were about to give up when one of the more robust youths said, "Let's try a little farther down, and let the old man know that we trust him."

Eleven feet. Finally, on the twelfth, they broke through to the water below. And what was more remarkable, their harpoons landed on the back of the whale.

There wasn't any question about their find. The escaping gas from that decomposing animal was nauseating.

Finally, they broke out a cake of ice 15 feet by 20 feet and 12 feet thick. They were then able to float the whale up to the surface. Its bloated condition helped to exhume it from its watery grave. Its meat was not what we would relish, but the crew made no fuss and ate it without comment.

THE KING ISLAND HUNT

One day papa set me down and told me about a hunting trip he took to King Island. This was to be a hunt for walrus. And he was to be entertained Alaskan style, staying overnight with an Eskimo family.

> Eskimos are famous for their hospitality. They will share their best to the last. The walrus hunt wasn't doing so well and the weather was threatening, so they decided to give their white visitor a real show. The entertainment began with a village dance.

My remembrance of the Eskimo dance, as a child, was terribly exciting and with their encouragement, I would often join them. The only place I have seen more rhythm or more violent activity in a dance was in the State of Punjab in North India. There, the farmers, all men, do a dance called the Bhangra. It is soul stirring with its heavy stomping and marching in circles. All with loud drum beats.

This little village of King Island was built on stilts, and their dance hall was built in a cave which in the past was used for a hideaway from enemy tribes.

King Island stilt village, May 1913

We entered through a long, low, subterranean tunnel until we came to an opening above our heads. We straightened up and put our heads and shoulders through a large hole. And spreading our arms on either side of the hole we lifted our bodies into a spacious room.

Driftwood planks along the walls, about three feet from the floor, provided seating for the men. The women and children sat in front of the men on the floor. Just enough room was left in the center of the room for the dancers.

A sky light made from the dried and stretched intestines of walrus gave some light from the outside. That, plus many little seal oil lamps, provided the light they needed for the party.

Water was passed to each drummer to moisten his skin drum. This was done to give the drums more resonance.

Skin percussion group accompanying dance, December 1912

Two muscular middle-aged men stripped to the waist started the dance. They came on their knees at first. Then, as the drum beats became louder, they slowly rose to their feet. Their arms took the

93

rhythm of the drums and they did a perfect exemplification of the motions of the seagull. At a certain signal from the drummers the men would shout, "Yah, yah, yah. Unga-yah, yah; e-yah, yah, yah!"

Eskimo traditional dance

These Eskimo on the Island are the most remarkable dancers I have seen in Alaska. Perfect rhythm. Perfect grace. Suppleness of the head rotating on the neck along with their smooth body and arm movements portrayed pictures of their world of nature.

94

Then the women came on.   Dancing always
separately from the men.   They were even more
graceful with their arms and knee bends than the
men.

Children dancing

When the dance was over a runner came in and
announced with some satisfaction that the weather
was still bad. "Don't you men want to tell stories?
I'm sure Mr. Van would be interested."

So, well into the night they were occupied with their
favorite pastime.   Many times the stories were
exaggerated as each one tried to out-tell the other.

Not to be outdone by my Eskimo friends, I began.

Let me tell you about the wonders of my great Outside world. Your lamps, as you know, are formed by using a piece of reindeer moss or a strip of calico for a wick pushing it up against the edges of a round, flat, open, soapstone dish. The dish is then filled with your seal oil. And I see here that you have done an ingenious thing to keep the fuel going with that piece of blubber hanging over the dish. I see that as the heat from the lamp melts the seal blubber, it continues to give fuel for your lamp indefinitely. You are very clever.

Now. Let me tell you about how people on the Outside world make light. All they have to do is push a button on the wall. The lights come on in little glass bottles corked so tightly that no oil or air can get inside. These lights can burn all night, all day, and many days if you don't push another button to turn them off.

We can talk over a wire from one igloo to another. People can talk to their friends many miles away. My Eskimo friends looked puzzled. "We believe what you say, but it is as a dream to us." One lad, not to be outclassed by my story, said, "There once lived a man with a big voice who lived in Miliktaik. He could call so loud that the people at Barrow eight miles away could hear him!"

At this time, Eskimos had no written language and the only way they had of preserving their history was to pass their stories on by word of mouth from one generation to another.   Fathers   to   sons. Mothers   to   daughters. And   as   I   have   listened   to their stories through the years I have been in the north, I have learned a lot about their history.

And so, Petungnak, the night passed. My hosts said with a smile that there would be time later for the walrus hunt.

ARCTIC WILD LIFE

"The astounding abundance of wild life in this region," writes my father in the 1920s, "may well be the envy of hunters everywhere." Young Tommy Brower, a lad of 14 years, boasted that he shot down 28 king eider ducks with one shot from his shot gun. Another man from Wainwright by the name of Gregg told of shooting down 70 Brant with his ten-gauge shot gun.

But, to be able to knock down whole flocks of eiders without firing a shot was the way the old Eskimo did it. They went hunting when the frost smoke was in the air. This smoke rising from the open leads in the ice was heavy and dark. At this time, ducks fly low where the moisture from the water is rising. This slows them down considerably.

The hunters wait on the beach until they see the flock thicken and then sneak out to the open water under the flight pattern where they hide behind ice hummocks. At a given signal, they break away from their hiding places and shout, "Hoy-hoyt!" They jump. They clap. They whistle, and make as much noise as they can. With just a second of pause in the air, the ducks, heavy with frost as well as their own extra winter fat, drop down on the ice. Some, because of their body fat, split open. Some break their necks. Others, more active, are picked up and the neck wringing process is a quick death.

Still other stories are told of geese arriving in their usual migration schedule before the snow and ice are melted. They land on a pond where there is some surface water, and because they are so tired they put their heads under their wings and go to sleep. A sleep from which they do not waken. For their feet soon freeze into the ice slush, and as the night comes on the temperatures drop and their feet are firmly frozen into the pond's surface.

Hunters come early before the sun is able to melt the ice to free the birds, and the Eskimo simply pick up their game, one by one. Ptarmigan seem to have the greatest ability to survive the intense cold of the Arctic. They are able to endure weeks of temperatures ranging from 40 to 60 degrees below zero in heavy blizzards. They found a way of burying themselves in the snow. A soft snowbank is located and they dive into it headfirst, go as deep as they can, and remain until the temperatures moderate.

Papa tells of walking through snow without a sign of life and suddenly with a WHIRRRRR and a BURRRRR-whizzzzz, in a cloud of snow, a flock of ptarmigan would take wing. Their camouflage is perfect, for in winter their feathers turn white to match their surroundings. And in summer their feathers brown against the colors of the tundra.

Water birds called snipes and red-throated phalarope walk along the beaches and are good game for the children. We used to catch them with nets like butterfly nets. I had a small wood burning stove, and when the children caught a snipe or two, we would de-feather them, clean out the innards, and cook them on the little stove right there on the beach. A picnic, Eskimo style.

The animals which survive in this part of the world are of necessity wise and sensitive to the rigors of their environment. The Arctic fox is a good example. He spends part of his life on land and part on the sea. On land, he stalks ducks, ptarmigan, geese, mice, lemming and eggs. He caches them for his "rainy day." Some instinct allows him to find them again, even after heavy snows have covered them.

At sea, he has learned to follow the polar bear to eat what the bear has left. The bear eats the fat of the seal and walrus, so that most of the meat is left for the fox. In winter, the fox's fur is white. And, like the ptarmigan, his coat turns blue-gray to blend with the summer colors.

The old Eskimo had ways of catching fox which were complicated, using deadfalls and snares. Of course, these are outdated now by the steel trap which the white man introduced. So effective have the new ways of trapping become that the fox, plentiful in those days, are now an endangered species.

ARCTIC FISH

The lakes and streams of the North abound in fine fish. In the 1920s they used hoop nets at the entrance of lakes when the fish were in migration. In summer, smelt were caught at night just by scooping them up in buckets from the water along the beaches.

In winter, the Eskimo dug holes in the thick ice. Sometimes several feet down. A whale bone line was used because any other line they might use would be covered with a new coat of ice each time it was pulled out of the hole. The weight of the layers of ice then could break the line. But, they found that whale bone lines seemed to shed the ice very well.

Their hooks were made from fossilized ivory and carved so as to resemble a worm. A nail was put through the ivory and bent backwards. There were no other barbs so that the fish could be shaken off the hook without removing their hands from mittens, a very important consideration when the temperatures are so cold.

The Eskimo made leaders from the quills of geese and cranes. No bait was used; however, fancy lures might be fastened on the backs of the hooks.

Nixies are a small fish but one of our favorites. We used to fry them whole and very crisp. Many times I have heard Papa exclaim as he fried them, "They smell just like fresh cucumbers." We ate them, bones and all. A good fishing day in winter would be a gunny sack full. Our ice cellar would store all those we couldn't eat right away, and they would keep as fresh as the day they were caught down

there, in our ice cellar — which never melted, summer or
winter.

An Eskimo woman with a good catch

MY DOG, ROSCOE

The Arctic husky is a vicious, wolf-like dog. He is intelligent. He can endure great changes in temperature. I have seen huskies buried in snow when the 50-degree-below-zero blizzards blew in from the sea. They are loyal and they are obedient to their masters.

But a little white girl was strange to them, and I was always warned to stop short of their leash lengths. Papa was worried, and decided that I should have a guard dog.

On one of our trips to the "Outside", my grandfather Barnhart gave me a big white collie. We named him Roscoe. He became my constant companion. He excelled in his job, and did very well for the most part. So well did he try to guard me that one day when he was hitched to my small sled, he dashed out after some huskies who were coming too near. He upset my sled and the steel runners came crashing across my nose. It broke. I carried that black and blue mark on the bridge of my nose for years.

My dog Roscoe

I am told that the Alaskan dog teams are almost passé now. They have been replaced by motorized vehicles. Part of our Northland is gone!

The April 1913, All-Alaskan Sweepstakes winner. Johnson's racing dogs at Sinuk, 26 miles from Nome. Perhaps the beginning of the present Iditarod race

Olive's arctic team

"Mushers"--ready for a dog team trip

Many stories have come out of the Arctic telling tales of hunters who were lost in blizzards who would drop the lines, freeing their teams to use their instincts of direction – and the dogs would find their way home.

Modernization of the Arctic is inevitable. But I am sad at the passing of the husky.

I wonder if the hunter isn't a little less safe.

THE MOSQUITO

A history of the Arctic just wouldn't be complete without the story of the mosquito.

Papa tells about a trip he took across the tundra to the Bitterroot mountains.

> We were made wretched by an unusually vicious onslaught of mosquitoes. My companion that day posed a question I have never been able to answer, "What him good for?" They are so thick sometimes on the Arctic slope that they form gray clouds over the ground. The creases in our trousers were filled with the dead ones. I have seen an offshore wind blow them into the sea in such numbers that the water appeared to be covered with foam.
>
> The reindeer go wild and stampede into the sea at times to get rid of them. Dogs' noses are especially vulnerable. The Eskimo use duck and goose wings to fan them away. I am told that the life of a mosquito is two to three months, but I swear, after tormenting deer, dogs and humans all summer, they

hibernate in the snow and ice. This is the truth. We have thawed them out of our drinking water which has been frozen all winter. And as each leg is thawed, it begins to wiggle. And then, we have seen them fly off to torment animals and humans for another season!

The mosquito. "What him good for?"

Our mail carrier and his team arriving at Wainwright from Kotzebue, May 1915

CHRISTMAS ABOVE THE ARCTIC CIRCLE

The following description from Papa's diary captures his love of this country. You feel it keenly as you read.

> Far up on the northern rim of the world where the wash of the Arctic Ocean has long since been hushed by heavy ice extending miles out to sea, the animals and birds of passage have all departed from this frost-bound land. Solitude reigns supreme, except when broken by the occasional howls of the huskies.
>
> Arctic midnight prevails even at midday, for the crimson sun that slipped below the southern horizon on November 17, will not be seen again before January 17. There is a strange co-mingling of light from the stars, moon, and aurora borealis. We are eight hundred miles north of our nearest white neighbors.

It is Christmas. And it is 47 degrees below zero. One hundred and fifty Eskimo guests are invited. They will come. It takes more than cold to keep them away from such a celebration as Christmas, even though they know little about the holiday.

Hours of complicated dancing and feasting filled the three days previous to the Christmas planned by their friend, Mr. Van Valin. Papa wanted them to know just how Christmas was celebrated in the States. The schoolhouse was the largest building in town. The men removed all the seats so more people could be accommodated on the floor. In one corner Papa built a little house with paper windows and doors and a big red brick-like chimney dropping down to an open fireplace.

All things seemed pretty much in order when Papa suddenly became aware that he didn't have a Christmas tree. "My goodness Olive, we don't have a tree. Where can we find a Christmas tree on this barren tundra?"

At the time of the reindeer roundup there were frequent horn fights, and they had stashed a lot of horns in the schoolhouse. Papa, always ready to try something new, said, "I'll find a 4 inch by 4 inch plank. I think there's one about 12 feet long in the closet. I'll nail the horns on it and see if it won't pass for a Christmas tree." The tinsel and baubles of Christmas covered those horn branches perfectly. We didn't miss the traditional evergreen at all.

Parenthetically, this tree later became a roosting place for the eight hens and one rooster we took north for fresh eggs. A sad tale follows. When the sun never set those two summer months, the hens layed themselves to death. And Mr. Rooster, well — he overdid too!

But for that unique Christmas, Papa's tree was placed near the fireplace of the little house where Santa Claus was to appear. All was ready. The crowd was seated and told to be quiet.

1913 Christmas in the Arctic

Across the tundra came the sound of the jingle bells of Santa Claus. He was coming with his reindeer and sled loaded with goodies for the people. At last the jolly old fellow danced into the schoolhouse ringing his bells.

Eskimo Santa and his reindeer

What a strange fellow he was. The Eskimo had never seen anyone like him. His white beard and his long white hair with red cap and suit were something they had never witnessed before. Yet, he spoke with a dialect they understood and he seemed a bit familiar to them. He laughed a lot, and everyone began laughing with him as he shouldered his heavy pack and climbed the ladder behind the house where his bag came tumbling down the chimney into the fireplace. It was ready to be opened and Santa, with Papa's help, passed out all the gifts. Everyone was remembered, children as well as adults - all 150 of them.

"Loaded" antler tree. Santa was very busy

When Santa finally took off his beard and hat, the Eskimo recognized him as Mr. Van's interpreter, Frank Seelameoo. And they laughed and laughed, for Eskimo laugh a lot.

And another feast was prepared by the women who, all year, had saved delicacies such as fish, eider ducks, ptarmigan, wild geese, choice cuts of whale meat and walrus which were either preserved in seal oil or just frozen.

Thus, with a wonderful celebration which civilization on the "Outside" might envy, our Christmas at Wainwright came to an end.

Mother Eskimo. Cape Prince of Wales c 1917

MOTHER ESKIMO

I saw her and visited with her in her humble hut made of willows and moss-covered tundra slabs. Her babe had been taken from under her parka (fur coat) next to her bare back and brought around under the fur garment to her breast without the babe being exposed to the cold at all. A seal oil lamp heated and lighted the dark room. Piles of fur skins were stashed in the background; bedding against the cold of the night. I marvel as I think of these primitive people at Barrow in the early 1900s, before the oil invasion and how they survived the 50 and 60 degree below zero temperatures.

Eskimo babes in those days wore no diapers. How those mothers kept them clean, I will always wonder. I remember in church they would take the little tikes out from under their parkas and set them between their legs over a tin can, give a little stimulation with Mother's hands, and take care of the tee-tee.

The oldest couple in Barrow and parents of Patkotak, Papa's interpreter. August 1913

The Eskimo mother was the meat man. She carved up the seal and walrus as they were brought in from the hunt.

Mother was the tailor. She made the fur pants and outer garments the whole family wore. She even made the boots and shoes. She made the thread from the intestines of the animals they hunted. She twisted and fastened together with her saliva the long strong strands with which she sewed even the water-proofed garments. The sole of the kumiks (boots) was chewed into tiny accordion pleats around the sole, so that the pleats made a standing border about an inch high. She used her teeth so much for this that, as she grew older, her teeth wore down to the gums. Sometimes the teeth were barely visible.

Eskimo morals were rigid. There was no wife-swapping in that country then. And I don't remember ever seeing an unhappy Eskimo mother. I am sure she must have had some bad days. But she worked HARD. And it was a continual battle to survive the hardships and the intense cold and raise her family. Perhaps, because she was so busy, she didn't require the care of a psychiatrist or marriage counselor. There weren't any up there, anyway.

A CHANCE MEETING

On one of Papa's teaching furloughs from Wainwright, Alaska, he decided to tour the state of California. So, we bundled up in an old Model T touring car rented from the Ford Company and set out for a three-week vacation. Above the license plate he attached a pennant "Alaska."

We hadn't gone too far when one of the front tires blew out and Papa pulled off to the side of the road. He barely got started jacking up the wheel when an old Jewett pulled alongside and the man behind the wheel hollered, "How about some help?" This fellow was from India over here on a furlough from a Mission project in Umri, Central India.

Those two fellows, one from the Far North and one from the other side of the world, had a great time changing that tire. While three children from one car and one from the other played tag and chewed on candy bars, the Moms talked women talk, and the men exchanged stories of whaling expeditions and tiger hunts.

Years went by. This episode was all but forgotten by both men.

In the halls of a small Junior College one day, two displaced freshmen met. The girl was from Alaska and the boy, from India. That first meeting, the boy declares to this day, he made up his mind that he would marry that dark-haired lass who reminded him of his first love in India. He was a British-educated chap with an accent that outdid Churchill. He looked the part too, with his high-water pants and his British hair parted in the middle.

American youths were sporting bell-bottom cords so "dirty they could stand alone", so the boys boasted.

She was trying hard to drop her Eskimo accent and educate her Eskimo trained feet to toe OUT, rather than to toe IN as the Eskimo did. She was trying, oh so hard, to become an all-American girl. So she wasn't enamored with the British fellow. Her father didn't like the idea either, for he would remind her through her college years that she could have a promising career in music if only she would stay in America.

It took six years for love to win. But in the end, Father Casberg's son, who was a passenger along with his two sisters in that car from India, married the daughter of William Van Valin, the explorer from Pt. Barrow, Alaska. There began, for these two young people, an adventure into the unknown through thirty major moves for Olive and Mel, in and out of four professions with tours of duty in several Asian countries.

"Yes, Mel, wherever or whatever, even India"

Dad lost his battle and his dream for his daughter to become a music professional when he realized that she was beginning to share Mel's dream of returning to his native land of India.

But my father was a good loser.

He followed with interest and sympathy as we struggled through the depression years for Mel's medical education and residency in surgery. And his admiration grew stronger as he followed our careers in other lands in service to other less fortunate people.

I guess that chance meeting on the roads of California was foreordained.

We must have been meant for each other.
After 57 years I am sure of it!

THE DIGGINGS

Twenty hundred years! Yes, two thousand years, and possibly more, they lay in their frozen confines.

How did it happen? What could have caused this holocaust? We wonder, perhaps an earthquake buried them while they slept. Maybe an Ice Pompeii covered the village.

There, on the coast of Alaska, on the outskirts of Barrow, an entire village of 83 prehistoric people were dug out of solid ice. My father, the archeologist, was commissioned to unbury them, one by one. It took him three years.

Then the question; how old could they be without a sign of the domestic dog or of any kind of metal? Their only tools were made of flint. It was finally determined that they had been buried all at once. They lay in their beds under fur blankets. All seemed free of disease.

Twenty-eight men were excavated here. The furry residue is polar bear skin bedding which covered their bodies

When I was eight years old I remember sitting by my father's side as he peeled away the flesh from one of the better preserved skulls and dropped it into formaldehyde solution immediately, lest it disintegrate in the air. For most of the flesh fell from the bones before the bodies could be removed from their icy graves.

Ootoyak, dad's digger, rests beside a pre-historic man encased in ice turned on edge to thaw. Covering his body was a perfectly preserved eider duck skin ateegee

Papa brought out 60 of these prehistoric skeletons to the Wistar Institute in Philadelphia. There they were to be studied as to the origin of the Eskimo. Papa had always felt that those on the coast of Alaska had come across the Bering Straits. His papers disclose the following account:

> My archeological investigations for the Wanamaker Expedition began at Pegnik, site of the oldest village known to the present-day Eskimos of northwest Alaska. The village was abandoned many years ago on account of the subsidence of the land, which permitted the influx of the ocean at high tide and during the offsea storms. Here, I collected numerous relics; but the greatest antiquarian discovery was found by chance.
>
> Ootoyuk, one of my employees, made the great find in a mound of earth eight miles south of Barrow. Eskimos had been hunting, trapping and camping over these half dozen mounds for generations. But these were a little different from the others. They were small glacial depositions scattered over the Arctic slope. Ootoyuk began to dig one day and struck ice. Then, FEATHERS! Then, he saw an ateegee (coat) of eider duckskin! He stopped in our cabin one day to see me, "Mr. Van, I think you should come to see what I found down the coast."
>
> "Perhaps later, Ootoyuk, when the sun shines warmer, we could explore it." But I was getting curious, and even as I put my friend off, I thought, this could be something special.
>
> "Wait, Ootoyuk, I have changed my mind. I will go with you immediately."

They outfitted an oomiak with food, cooking utensils, tents, picks and shovels and sailed into a snow storm down the coast to Pegnik. Weather couldn't stop them now. They packed their equipment a thousand feet up a draw where the tides couldn't reach them and began a careful excavation of three years duration. Ootoyuk HAD discovered something very SPECIAL.

The snow lessened. The wind died down. And they found several more mounds. These ranged in size from fifteen feet square to fifteen by forty-five feet. Papa said his curiosity was unbounded. And he marveled at what a revelation of centuries he might find underneath those curious mounds only five feet above ground.

They proceeded to pitch a permanent camp. Work began right away. First, the decomposed vegetation which had been accumulating for a long, long time had to be cleared. Beneath the deposit of vegetation they struck ice. And beneath the ice, a heap of bear skins.

Papa's comments on the dig go on:

> Chipping at the ice was like sticking a pick in rubber. Ice and fur were so matted that the pick wouldn't go through.
>
> The bones we first uncovered were two large and rounded ones which were colored red from oxidation.
>
> "Nunuk, nunuk!" shouted Ootoyuk. (bear, bear). "No, I replied, "innyuk!" (a man).
>
> The body was lying on his back with his heels drawn up against his buttocks. "Oomalik! Oomalikbuk!" (he is a big chief). I agreed. And as more of his frame was uncovered we both said, "Azera, oomalikbukbuk!" (great big chief).
>
> Then what a task to remove him! We found it necessary to dig straight down beyond the edge of the bearskin, and then undercut until we were able with well-directed blows to split the icy sarcophagus loose and turn it up on edge where the sun could melt the ice covering the cadaver.
>
> Beside him we were surprised to find a diminutive woman.
>
> Of the 83 bodies that were disintered this first man was the largest. Much larger than any Eskimo we had known.

There were infants clad in swaddling clothes made of cub bearskins. There were old Eskimo women who had worn their teeth to the gums in pleating the komiks. There were what we identified as old men who had lost all their teeth. And only ONE person in the whole lot had gray hair.

We invited many of the curious Eskimos to come and look at the findings. We were anxious not to offend them. They asked a lot of questions. And we asked if anyone could recall in their legends or stories passed on from one generation to the other, some remembrance of these buried people. But no one knew anything about them.

Some of the bodies were clad in ateegees (coats) made from fowl and animal skins. Some were of polar bearskin, some of seal skin and fox. Most of the bodies lay on beds of willows and moss. Their bedding consisted of brown bearskin, polar bearskin and musk ox. We found no trace of caribou skin so commonly used now. However, we found what we thought were caribou bones which were used for different instruments.

We kept wondering how these people had met their death. There were no signs of violence. Some had wooden drinking tubes in their hands. Others had blubber sticks with which they probably had fed themselves from a nearby whalebone vessel. That whalebone container still had pieces of seal flipper, meat and blubber!

One corpse had a three-pronged fish spear in his hand. Some had their arms down by their sides, and some had their arms folded peacefully across their breasts. We felt their positions suggested that they had clung to life tenaciously and had tried to keep from freezing by covering themselves with all the furs they owned. Some even had their heads pulled back into their fur hoods.

Papa's unusual tale goes on:

We examined every adult to find evidence of the tutuk (labret). Tutuk is a piece of wood or ivory inserted in holes which the Eskimo cut in their lower cheeks or across the lower lip. Evidently that practice hadn't been introduced to them. Perhaps, it came to them later from the primitive split-lipped Indian women of southeastern Alaska.

The custom is a strange streak of vanity, really, for when the ivory or bone ornament is left out, drinking soup or eating fat meat is awkward. Either a couple of trickles of seal oil or blood from the uncooked meat drips out and down from the chin. So, I asked them one day why they do it, and the reply was "Areega!" (it's pretty).

Again, we were surprised to find no trace of copper or any other metallic substance. These people, we decided, must be of the stone age culture. It's hard to imagine them carving a boat frame or a dog sled with a sharpened stone, flint or jadeite. Their cooking and eating pots were made of whale bone or clay and evidence of molding and burning the clay pots was found. And how they made fire is another mystery.

There was no tobacco then. Perhaps that came to Alaska with the first white man. We found no evidence that these people had dogs.

WHEN, HOW, AND WHY these prehistoric people met their death is still a deep mystery. Perhaps, they fell victim to ptomaine poisoning. Perhaps their frozen world kept them from hunting food and they starved to death. Or, perhaps, some epidemic struck. Who can tell.

Exhuming those ancient bodies was a disagreeable task for several reasons, the worst of which was the odor of putrefied human flesh, especially when the weather was warm. As each was exposed to the air, disintegration set in rapidly. It was so bad sometimes that we tried as we dug, to stand on the windward side. Even then, the Eskimo workers were really frightened to be so close to the dead. Some predicted dire tragedy if we continued to dig. They would threaten with, "Maybe the weather would be so bad that the ice wouldn't let the ships in to Barrow next spring." They warned, "Oh, there are ways of punishment for those who disturb the dead."

Actually as spring arrived, we were afraid the old Eskimo were right, for the season was about to end before the ships ventured into the open leads to Barrow. And all because they felt we had disturbed the graves of their ancestors.

So, we had to hurry when the ice did move, to get our freight ready to ship. It was terribly important to get this unusual find to the Outside.

That last trip from Barrow was full of adventure. Our ship followed an open lead through the ice for sixty miles with the threat of being crushed from each side by moving ice. Once we got through that we ran into snow squalls and fog.

TERRIBLE, blinding fog. I got my first intense feeling of TERROR from fog that day on the boat when I came on deck and spotted a line of breakers straight ahead. I called frantically to the First Mate, "We are headed into a line of breakers on some island shore!"

A shout from the First Mate, "All hands on deck. Emergency!" And men laid hold of the booms. The sails were swung to catch the offshore wind to aid the engines. The pilot spun his wheel hard over. And we narrowly missed sudden disaster on that desolate island!

Passing the two Diomede Islands finally, we regained the course from which we had drifted. And when we reached Cape Prince of Wales, we found that the Bering Sea was running like a millrace. Currents were going wild. But again we weathered that last treacherous race with nature, and the rest of our voyage was calm.

Papa writes, "Returning to civilization we find ourselves rich in knowledge and experience, and laden with bones of sixty prehistoric Eskimo, a forty-five hundred piece collection of Eskimo treasures from the past, together with ten thousand feet of motion picture film of that fascinating and little-known region of the world."

I am sad that Papa died not knowing how very old his diggings were. They now have been carbon dated two thousand years old. The Museum of the University of Pennsylvania has honored him at their centenary celebration this year in the publication of "Raven's Journey" in which they have printed his pictures of many of the antiquities found in that village buried two thousand years ago!

The Point Hope graveyard within a whale-rib fence

Tundra block houses at Point Hope Village, August 1913. Translucent skylights are urine-tanned entrails

Claud Kataktovick, Captain Bartlett's Eskimo traveling companion from Wrangel Island over the ice to the Siberian coast. He had been a member of the Karlucks crew of the 1916 Vilhjalmur Stefansson Expedition. Their ship was carried from Point Tangent south-east of Point Barrow in a large field of ice where she was crushed. Captain Bartlett led the crew to safety

"Adrift twenty-five miles off the Alaskan coast. Two Eskimo hunters scan the sea for pack ice. This is a perilous position for melting cakes may turn over unexpectedly"

PAPA'S OWN PICTURE OF HIS BELOVED NORTHLAND

To him, Alaska was the most beautiful part of the world. His appreciation of the "Top of the world", as he called it, knew no bounds. I quote again from his diary describing the beauty of the simple, natural formation of drinking water from salty sea water.

> My Arctic presents such beauty even in the making of drinking water from the sea.
>
> When sea water freezes the salt content precipitates in two directions. That which is on the surface freezes in a semislushy condition. And, as this slush thickens, the saline part grows into salt crystals about the size of fingers. Then, they begin to cluster and rise to two or three inches high.
>
> When the midnight sun shines through these clusters it creates a field of Arctic diamonds. Imagine quintillions of crystals scintillating with all the prismatic hues of the rainbow!

The surpassing beauty and mystical setting of the midnight sun

I have traversed this gorgeous garden in bitterly cold weather, kicking as I went and making a clinking, shattering sound like the breaking of fine glass. I called it the music of salt water ice converting itself into our pure and unsalty drinking water.

Looking over the sparkling luminous highway, so gloriously radiant under the midnight sun, I thought, how few mortals ever see this beauty! And, I remembered Gray's lines:

"Full many a gem of purest ray serene
The dark unfathomed caves of ocean bear;
Full many a flower is born to blush unseen
And waste its sweetness on the desert air."

Life beneath this midnight sunlight is bewitchingly charming.

The top of a pressure ridge is an ideal place from which to gain a breath-taking perspective. It is a rugged climb and I have done it several times alone. The view is unforgettable. At twelve midnight, by the clock, the crimson sun appears over the horizon through a rift in a fiery profusion of clouds whose blazing streamers radiate fanwise over half the heavens. As far as the eye can see, to where land and sky meet, there is no one visible in any direction. Just a vacant, ice-locked plain with its once smooth floor, now disrupted and shattered into a chaotic confusion of ridges, hummocks and gorges. The crags are touched with rays of pure silver and gold.

The wind is still.

Not a sound can be heard in all this vastness except the beat of one's own heart.

Sometimes, perfect silence is startling. Instead of being negative, it becomes a positive thing.

And I thought again, "What a shrine this would be for the worshipper of nature."

Let the haughty mortal overproud of his accomplishments, wealth or general greatness, climb to the summit of my mighty ridge, let him stand on a single fragment of ice as large as a house, take in as much as he can scan of this stilled expanse of immense white solitude. Then, let him see if he can find himself – an infinitesimal speck on the face of creation.

Let him STOP. THINK!

Otherwise important or prized possessions are valueless. I have been in places where the combined riches of Fords and Rockefellars would have been worthless. Where a single match was of more importance than a whole world of money.

We returned to civilization enriched in knowledge and experience, having made many lasting friendships among our beloved Eskimo.

My archeological investigation for the Wanamaker Expedition was over!

What can I say about a man so imaginative and resourceful? So willing to venture into Arctic wastes, live under primitive conditions with the natives of the North who became closer to him than his own brothers and sisters.

I wish to God I could say he made a good adjustment as he returned to the "Outside." My heart ached at times, watching as he tried to fit into our society again.

Peter Jenkins who wrote in his book, *Across China*: "Once you get used to living at intense levels always with the possibility of death close by, it's hard to check back into normal life again."

On one of our recent trips to the Arctic, I found this written on a plaque. I had to buy it, for it was so apropos to my Papa's life:

> Once you've gone to Alaska,
>
> You never come ALL THE WAY BACK.

He lectured all over our country. He wrote about his adventures in the North. And he published both in England and the U.S. Always about his favorite place in the world.

HIS HEART REMAINED IN THE WILDS OF ALASKA.

Papa's last request was for me to put down on paper the melodies of his ballads which he had sung throughout his life. He had all of them memorized, but they had never been put in print.

"Would you harmonize them too, Olive dear?"

I am glad I did, if only for him.

I went to India.

He went HOME.

Heaven, I know.

And I know his heaven is a little like Alaska:

A heaven of a billion snow diamonds

Glistening in never ending sunlight!

POSTLUDE

Years slipped by. Arthritis took its toll on mother.

A stroke partially blinded her at age 84. We sought out a comfortable, complete care home where she was among friends and her own kin.

Twice each month we made the trip from a beach city to Los Angeles to give her the shots she required to keep her arthritic pains controlled. But the habits of a lifetime only become exaggerated as one ages. And happiness eluded her.

One evening, I decided, intuitively, to go alone for a quiet visit with mother. I took with me Dad's collection of songs. "Mother, I thought you might like to hear some of Dad's music tonight. I'll tuck you in so you can go to sleep if you like while I go to the piano and sing for you."

I sang for more than an hour. When I finished, she was drowsy. I kissed her forehead and bid her goodnight.

Two days later, I was called from my church pew during the morning worship hour. Mother was gone.

The music I sang that evening was a healing thing. I gave her the knowledge that I held nothing against her. At the same time, I gave her the opportunity to seek forgiveness as well.

As I sang, I remembered, through tears, the times my father used those very songs as a balm to heal the hurts which plagued our family in the years we lived together.

****